DEEPWATER HORIZON OIL SPILL

UNNATURAL DISASTERS

T0027031

JULIE KNUTSON

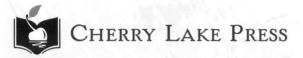

Published in the United States of America by Cherry Lake Publishing Group
Ann Arbor, Michigan
www.cherrylakepublishing.com

Reading Adviser: Marla Conn, MS, Ed., Literacy specialist, Read-Ability, Inc.
Photo Credits: © forestpath/shutterstock.com, cover, 1; © EPI2oh/Photo by US Coast Guard/flickr, 5;
    © Steve Buissinne/Pixabay, 9; © Photo Mix/Pixabay, 10; © Deepwater Horizon Response/Photo by US Coast
    Guard Petty Officer 1st Class Sara Francis/flickr, 12; © Florida Fish and Wildlife/Photo by Tim Donovan/
    FWC/flickr, 16, 20; © NASA Goddard Space Flight Center/Photo courtesy of the MODIS Rapid Response
    Team/flickr, 19; © Louisiana GOHSEP/Photo courtesy of LA Department of Wildlife and Fisheries/flickr, 23;
    © Louisiana GOHSEP/Photo courtesy of Governor Jindal's Office/flickr, 24; © NOAA and Georgia Department
    of Natural Resources, 26

Cherry Lake Press is an imprint of Cherry Lake Publishing Group.

Library of Congress Cataloging-in-Publication Data
Names: Knutson, Julie, author.
Title: Deepwater Horizon oil spill / Julie Knutson.
Description: Ann Arbor, Michigan : Cherry Lake Publishing, 2021. | Series: Unnatural disasters : human
    error, design flaws, and bad decisions | Includes index. | Audience: Grades 4-6 | Summary: "Human
    modification of the environment always carries a risk of accident and folly. Explore the causes and
    consequences of the Deepwater Horizon oil spill in the Gulf of Mexico in 2010. Guided by compelling
    questions such as, "What led to this disaster?," "Who was impacted by it?," and "What changed in
    its aftermath?" the interdisciplinary content blends social studies and science. Ultimately, it pushes
    students to consider how humans can meet their need for resources in a safe, sustainable way. Books
    include table of contents, index, glossary, author biography, and timeline"—Provided by publisher.
Identifiers: LCCN 2020040033 (print) | LCCN 2020040034 (ebook) | ISBN 9781534180178 (hardcover) |
    ISBN 9781534181885 (paperback) | ISBN 9781534181182 (pdf) | ISBN 9781534182899 (ebook)
Subjects: LCSH: BP Deepwater Horizon Explosion and Oil Spill, 2010—Juvenile literature. | BP Deepwater
    Horizon Explosion and Oil Spill, 2010—Environmental aspects—Juvenile literature. | Oil spills—Mexico,
    Gulf of—Juvenile literature.
Classification: LCC TD427.P4 K58 2021 (print) | LCC TD427.P4 (ebook) |
    DDC 363.11/9622338190916364—dc23
LC record available at https://lccn.loc.gov/2020040033
LC ebook record available at https://lccn.loc.gov/2020040034

Cherry Lake Publishing Group would like to acknowledge the work of the Partnership for 21st Century
Learning, a Network of Battelle for Kids. Please visit http://www.battelleforkids.org/networks/p21
for more information.

Printed in the United States of America
Corporate Graphics

ABOUT THE AUTHOR

Julie Knutson is an Illinois-based author. In her spare moments, she enjoys investigating
new places and ideas alongside her husband, son, and border collie.

TABLE OF CONTENTS

INTRODUCTION

April 21, 2010. Look back at newspapers from this day, and you'll find hardly a hint that a major environmental catastrophe had begun the night before in the Gulf of Mexico. In St. Louis, a medical study on the health risks of salt made the front page. The lead story in the *Fort Worth Telegram-Star* was about biofuel-powered trains. And in Boston, journalists celebrated the homecoming of travelers whose return trips had been complicated by a lava-spewing volcano in Iceland.

The world wasn't yet aware of the massive oil **rig** explosion about 41 miles (66 kilometers) off the shore of Louisiana. People didn't know that 11 of the 126 workers on the drilling platform had died in the blast and that another 16 were injured. They didn't know that workers leapt into the Gulf as flames soared as high as a 15-story building. They didn't know that the entire platform would sink 2 days later.

On the night of April 20, 2010, at 10 p.m., a massive explosion happened about 41 miles (66 km) off the Louisiana Coast in the Gulf of Mexico.

The name *Deepwater Horizon* wasn't yet known to households across the world. On the morning of April 21, 2010, no one imagined that the largest human-caused environmental accident in U.S. history had begun.

In the 3 months that followed, the world watched in horror as the company that operated the platform, British Petroleum (BP), failed to cap the oil gushing from the ocean's floor. This oil spread. It sank to the bottom of the sea. It crept toward coastal beaches, wetlands, and **estuaries**. It slicked the surface of the water, in one area measuring *three times* the size of Rhode Island. It wreaked havoc on plant and animal life. And it threatened the very existence of our oceans, which United Nations Secretary-General António Guterres has called "the lungs of our planet."

Why did this happen? How was it stopped? What were its impacts? And can we guarantee that an accident like this never happens again?

Imagine 300 Olympic-sized swimming pools filled with slippery, midnight-black oil. That's the amount of crude oil that oozed out of the Deepwater Horizon *drill site between April and July 2010. Scientists are still studying the impacts of this massive spill on ocean and coastline ecosystems today.*

Prioritizing Ocean Health

"All life on Earth is dependent on a healthy ocean," notes marine biologist and *National Geographic* Explorer-in-Residence Sylvia Earle. "If the ocean is in trouble, we are in trouble."

Why do oceans matter? Oceans govern the carbon, oxygen, and water cycles. They regulate climate. They are home to more than half of all life-forms on the planet. Yet human choices continue to threaten ocean health. Whether from deepwater drilling, plastic pollution, or overfishing, the world's oceans are in danger. The United Nations (UN) Sustainable Development Goals make ocean health a priority with goal 14, "Life Below Water." In addition, the UN has declared the years 2021 through 2030 the Decade of Ocean Science for Sustainable Development, urging everyone to advocate and care for our oceans.

CHAPTER 1

Before

In 2006, 3,858 oil and gas platforms dotted the Gulf of Mexico. Then and today, these hulking complexes of metal and concrete loom high above the water. They're miniature islands designed to pump oil from the seafloor at depths of more than 5,000 feet (1,524 meters). How did humans end up going to these extremes to **extract** oil and natural gas?

With the **Industrial Revolution** came a growing need for petroleum. Some of the world's first offshore oil wells popped up off of the California coast in the late 1800s to meet industrial demands. The first freestanding offshore well in the Gulf of Mexico was built in 1938 in just 14 feet (4 m) of water.

[21ST CENTURY SKILLS LIBRARY]

Excavating, processing, and using fossil fuels affect the entire Earth from land degradation to water and air pollution.

In today's world, we use oil and gas to power factories, cars, and airplanes. These **fossil fuels** heat homes. They generate the electricity that powers phones, computers, and refrigerators. They show up in a range of other products, from deodorant to dish detergent. But fossil fuels are also **nonrenewable**. This means that the reserve of oil, coal, and gas locked in the Earth will someday run out. By current estimates, that seems likely to happen in the next 50 to 100 years.

There are policies and incentives in place that encourage people and companies to use renewable energy sources instead, like wind and solar power.

Human dependence on fossil fuels is complicated by politics, economics, and geography. Because the U.S. government wanted to reduce reliance on foreign oil, **subsidies** were offered to corporations exploring for oil in the Gulf of Mexico.

The need for cheap fuel led companies to drill in riskier places, including on the deep seafloor, with its crushing water pressure. Safety technology didn't advance as rapidly as new tools for extracting oil. In the rush to drill and cut costs, accident **protocols** sometimes went overlooked. Cleanup plans were poorly sketched.

Where Do Fossil Fuels Come From?

Fossil fuels, like coal and oil, are the remains of decomposed plants and animals that lived 300 million to 400 million years ago—well before the dinosaurs prowled the planet. Millions of years of compression and heat, paired with the action of microorganisms, produced these **hydrocarbons**.

While coal formed mainly from plants, oil emerged out of decomposed marine life. That's why oil reserves are often found in parts of the world that were once covered by water. Today, one-third of oil and gas extracted globally comes from offshore sources.

The oil spill was caused by failures, including a valve failing to seal, a misinterpretation of a pressure test, a leak left undetected, and a gas detection alarm failing.

The *Deepwater Horizon* rig was operated by BP. In the years leading up to this accident, BP's safety record was mixed. In March 2005, an explosion at BP's Texas City plant killed 15 people and left 170 others injured. For years, workers there had complained about rusted, corroded equipment. These complaints went unheard. The consequences were tragic, leading to the country's biggest industrial accident in decades.

In July of that same year, BP's *Thunder Horse* rig in the Gulf was toppled by Hurricane Dennis due to human error in plumbing. Around the same time, workers and contractors with BP in Alaska complained of aging **infrastructure** that could lead to pipeline ruptures. In March 2006, an oil leak was discovered. Over 5 days, the pipes bled 212,252 gallons (803,461 liters) of oil over 1.9 acres (0.8 hectares) in the Arctic. While penalties and fines were paid, these red flags went largely ignored. They paved the way to an even bigger ecological disaster.

According to the U.S. Energy Information Administration, about 63 percent of electricity generated in 2018 came from fossil fuels (coal, natural gas, petroleum, and other gases). Another 20 percent of energy came from nuclear sources and 17 percent from renewables like solar or wind power.

CHAPTER 2

The Accident

Over 87 days, more than 200 million barrels of oil seeped into the Gulf of Mexico. That's 99,700 gallons (377,406 L) per hour for a period of 3 months. Its effects on plants, animals, and people were felt immediately. Its effects linger today. What happened that caused this disaster? How did people respond? And why did it take so long to stop the seepage?

On April 20, everything that could go wrong did go wrong at the *Deepwater Horizon* drill site. While a crew worked to plug and close an exploratory well, a flare of gas ran up through a pipe that connected the platform to the deep seabed. A "blowout protector"— a valve to cap the well in an emergency and prevent a major spill— failed. The gas reached the rig, which exploded and was soon engulfed in flames. Other equipment that could have prevented the catastrophe by shutting off the well, like a sound-activated cutoff switch, weren't in place. This device was required for drilling projects elsewhere in the world but not in U.S. waters.

The Center for Biological Diversity assessed the Deepwater Horizon spill's impact on wildlife. Experts believe that it "harmed or killed about 82,000 birds . . . about 6,165 sea turtles; as many as 25,900 marine mammals; and a vast (but unknown) number of fish."

BP wasn't prepared for the disaster. Its plan for a potential spill in the Gulf—developed the year before—was deeply flawed. It cited sea lions and walruses as marine mammals that would be threatened by the accident. But the closest these critters can be found is on the country's Pacific coast. The plan also didn't include details of *how* to stop a deepwater blowout. BP was in uncharted territory. The company was relying on trial and error and on methods used decades earlier to fix an emergency that needed immediate attention.

The explosion polluted the Gulf of Mexico with about 200 million barrels (about 8.4 billion gallons or 31.8 billion liters) of oil.

By the morning of April 22, the spill was headline news. As the Coast Guard searched for the 11 missing workers, the massive drill structure sank, collapsing beneath the sea. However, even with the platform gone, the crude oil continued to leak. Attempts to stop the gusher and contain the oil began. But because of intense water pressure and frigid deepwater temperatures, a fix would be neither swift nor easy.

First, engineers tried "Operation Top Hat," which involved lowering a four-story containment dome on top of the well. It would sit on the well like—you guessed it—a top hat, and stem the oil flow. But as the dome was lowered, it got clogged by an icy slush. It didn't work. More efforts followed, with names that sounded straight from spy movies like "Operation Top Kill" and "Junk Shot." Junk Shot attempted to dump a mix of mud, tires, and rubber golf balls into the leak to curb the flow of oil. Then, the well would be sealed with cement. Both attempts were public failures.

As engineers tried to stop oil bleeding from the deepwater site, others focused on containing its spread at the surface. Dr. Carl Safina of the Blue Oceans Institute told a film crew that the surface of the Gulf looked as though there were "thick anacondas of oil snaking their way across the surface." The Coast Guard and **contracted** crews worked to collect the oil through skimming the surface and controlled burns. BP used another tactic: a chemical **dispersant** called Corexit.

BP's plan was to use the dispersant to speed up the decomposition of spilled oil into tiny droplets. These smaller droplets would be broken down even further by ocean bacteria and microorganisms. The choice of Corexit raised eyebrows worldwide. The chemical was banned in the United Kingdom and Europe because of its potential harm to humans. As a known toxin, Corexit could impact not only exposed emergency workers, but also the whole ocean food chain—from tiny plankton to massive sperm whales. It could settle in coral reefs and sand, impacting ocean **ecosystems** for unknown lengths of time.

At a July 10, 2010, hearing, Senator Barbara Mikulski of Maryland stated, "I don't want dispersants to be the **Agent Orange** of this oil spill, and I want to be assured, on behalf of the American people, that this is okay to use, and okay to use in the amounts that we're talking about."

Mississippi   Alabama   Florida

leak location •

The coasts of Florida, Mississippi, Alabama, Texas, and Louisiana—about 1,300 miles of shoreline (2,092 km)—were affected by the oil spill.

While congresspeople and Gulf Coast citizens alike raised alarm, BP continued to spray the dispersant across the water's surface. In all, BP used 2 million gallons (7.6 million L) of Corexit during the 3-month crisis.

By early June, 88,000 square miles (227,919 square kilometers) of federal fisheries in the Gulf were off-limits. People working in the fishing industry were suddenly unemployed. Concerns that the spill's effects might not just be temporary, but continue into the

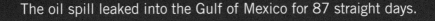

The oil spill leaked into the Gulf of Mexico for 87 straight days.

future, plagued area residents. The coast provides one-third of wild-caught seafood in the United States. As birds coated with oil were rescued and tar balls washed up on Florida's white sand beaches, people wondered what the lasting impact would be on themselves and the plants and animals around them.

[21ST CENTURY SKILLS LIBRARY]

On July 15, robots that could sustain the pressure of the deep waters managed to place a cement cap on top of the well. It seemed like the well was plugged. A few weeks later, BP began pumping mud and cement into the well to "kill" the leak. The process wasn't finished until mid-September, when the well was declared "officially dead" by retired U.S. Coast Guard admiral Thad Allen. The "underwater volcano of oil" had finally stopped.

There is one oil spill that surpassed Deepwater Horizon in magnitude, but it wasn't an accident. In 1991, Iraqi forces invaded Kuwait at the order of their president, Saddam Hussein. One of Iraq's aims was to acquire Kuwait's massive oil reserves. When Iraqi troops failed, they retreated and released a swell of oil into the Persian Gulf, with the goal of halting enemy marine troops from making landfall. Estimates of the amount of oil released in the Gulf War Oil Spill range from 380 million to 520 million gallons.

CHAPTER 3

After

It's been more than a decade since the *Deepwater Horizon* disaster. During and after the event, thousands of people worked to clean up shorelines and the Gulf's waters. The U.S. government set up new rules to protect oceans and coastal communities from spills. And BP paid more than $20 billion in damages and penalties. About $13 billion of BP's payout went to restoring ecosystems and researching the impact of the spill on the 1,300 miles (2,092 km) of contaminated coast. But the catastrophe didn't stop companies from drilling in the Gulf. In recent years, rigs have been working in even deeper waters. And since 2017, some safety **regulations** put in place after the accident have even been rolled back.

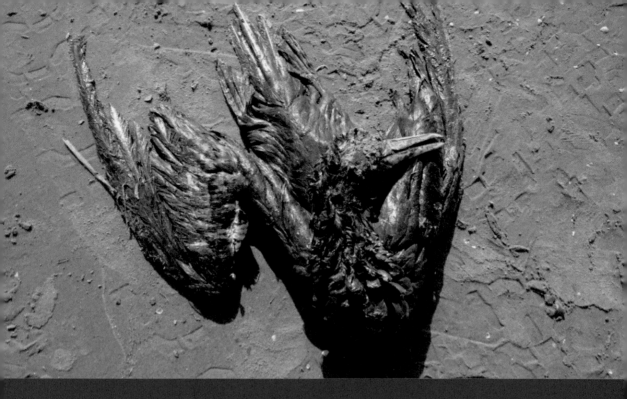

The effects of oil spills are devastating to animals that live in the area.

The short-term effects of *Deepwater Horizon* were evident to anyone living along the Gulf. There was the environmental toll on wildlife both on land and at sea. Biologists located "dead zones" near the spill site. In these oxygen-deprived stretches, fish and other ocean animals couldn't survive. One year after the accident, marine scientist Samantha Joye made multiple trips in the submarine *Alvin* to document damage to the seabed. At half-mile depths,

The Louisiana coast is approximately 400 miles (643.7 km), and of that, about 125 miles (201 km) were affected by the oil spill.

a brown-tinged layer of oil could be seen on the ocean's floor in all directions. Damage wasn't limited to the water. Along the coast, oil deposits in the soil were found to be 100 times higher than they had been 8 years earlier.

Oil on the ocean floor collected in sand and sediment, sucking oxygen needed to sustain life from the environment. The effects on reef fish diversity and other species continue to be noted more than a decade later. While oil concentrations along the coast have lessened, they are still 10 times what they should be. And although

[21ST CENTURY SKILLS LIBRARY]

conservationists have replanted reefs and restored ecosystems, it could take decades for full regrowth. The long-term health toll on workers exposed both to oil and dispersants also remains to be seen.

After the spill, it took the government time to develop new legislation and safety requirements. Under President Obama, the Bureau of Safety and Environmental Enforcement (BSEE) was created to monitor drilling practices. In 2016, the BSEE introduced new rules to prevent similar disasters, like regular inspections and safety checks. However, under President Trump, many of these protections have been rolled back on the grounds that the oil industry can "self-regulate."

The spill had major economic impacts too. The Gulf's seafood and tourist industries were hit especially hard. In Louisiana alone, visitor spending dropped by $247 million in 2010.

Despite the hazards, humans continue to count on offshore oil as an energy source, and oil companies are going to even greater depths to extract it. In 2010, *Deepwater Horizon* was considered a very deep well at 4,993 feet (1,522 m). Today, as *National Geographic* reports, "more than 50 percent of Gulf oil production comes from ultra-deep wells drilled in 4,500 feet [1,372 m] or more of water."

Many endangered animals, including sea turtles, were exposed to the oil spill.

With every 100 feet (30 m) further into the seabed that a well is drilled, the risk of accident or worker injury increases by 8 percent.

Oil may be a cheap energy source in the short term, but deepwater drilling carries risks. And the world's oil reserves will eventually run out. So is humankind's current reliance on oil worth it, given that another spill like *Deepwater Horizon* could happen? If we look to energy **transitions** of the past, we see that people moved from using wood to coal, and then from coal to oil. At this moment, we're on the cusp of moving toward cleaner, renewable energy sources, like wind, geothermal, and solar power.

Oil—and oil spills—aren't inevitable. For the sake of our oceans and climate, it is up to us to envision other possibilities for meeting energy needs.

Every year, World Oceans Day is celebrated on June 8. As the UN notes, "It is a day to celebrate together the beauty, the wealth, and the promise of the ocean."

Research & Act

Honor the world's oceans by making a public service announcement (PSA) about their importance. Educate family, friends, and classmates with this PSA. You can also promote everyday actions that people can take to protect "Life Below Water" (Sustainable Development Goal 14).

Here are just a few suggested actions that you can take starting now, courtesy of the UN:

- Volunteer to clean up waterways, beaches, and shorelines.

- Don't buy jewelry or other items made from coral, tortoise shells, or other marine life.

- Support organizations that protect the oceans.

- Use less plastic—it often ends up polluting oceans and waterways.

- Conserve water and energy—only use the dishwasher or laundry machine if full.

- Learn more by watching documentaries and reading about the value of ocean ecosystems.

Timeline

March 23, 2005: An explosion at BP's Texas City refinery kills 15 workers and injures 170 others.

March 2, 2006: An oil leak is discovered along BP's Prudhoe Bay pipeline in Alaska.

April 20, 2010: The *Deepwater Horizon* rig explodes in the Gulf of Mexico, killing 11 workers.

April 22, 2010: The rig sinks into the Gulf's waters.

April 30, 2010: Oil from the spill begins washing up on the Louisiana coast.

May 26, 2010: BP officials try to plug the leak with a heavy drilling mud in "Operation Top Kill," but fail.

July 15, 2010: BP announces that the oil leak has been controlled.

September 19, 2010: The well is declared "effectively dead" by a U.S. Coast Guard official.

2016: Congress enacts new laws for monitoring the safety of offshore drilling.

May 2019: The Trump administration rolls back regulations created to prevent similar disasters.

Further Research

Goldish, Meish. *Oil Spill: Deepwater Horizon.* New York, NY: Bearport Publishing, 2018.

Landau, Elaine. *Oil Spill! Disaster in the Gulf of Mexico.* Minneapolis, MN: Millbrook Press, 2011.

Leavitt, Amie Jane. *Life in the Gulf of Mexico.* Kennett Square, PA: Purple Toad Publishing, 2018.

Orr, Tamra. *BP Oil Spill and Energy Policy.* Ann Arbor, MI: Cherry Lake Publishing, 2018.

Stone, Adam. *The Deepwater Horizon Oil Spill.* Hopkins, MN: Bellwether Media, Inc., 2016.

Glossary

Agent Orange (AY-juhnt OR-inj) a highly toxic chemical used by the United States during the Vietnam War

contracted (KAHN-trakt-id) hired for a set amount of time to do a specific job

dispersant (dis-PURS-uhnt) a liquid or gas chemical used to break apart a substance

ecosystems (EE-koh-sis-tuhmz) the plants and animals that make up a biological system

estuaries (ES-choo-er-eez) the wide parts of a river where they join the ocean

extract (ek-STRAKT) to remove or pull something out

fossil fuels (FAH-suhl FYOO-uhlz) natural fuels such as coal or gas, formed out of the remains of living organisms

hydrocarbons (HYE-droh-kahr-buhnz) compounds made up of hydrogen and carbon that are the main elements of natural gas and oil

Industrial Revolution (in-DUHS-tree-uhl rev-uh-LOO-shuhn) a large social and economic shift toward machine and factory-produced goods

infrastructure (IN-fruh-struht-chur) the items needed to successfully run a business or operation

nonrenewable (nahn-rih-NOO-uh-buhl) not able to be replaced because there is a limited amount

protocols (PROH-tuh-kawlz) set processes that are followed

regulations (reg-yuh-LAY-shuhnz) rules

rig (RIG) a structure used to drill oil

subsidies (suhb-SID-eez) government financial assistance to a company or organization

transitions (tran-ZISH-uhnz) moves made from one thing to another

INDEX